LANDSCAPES
OF THE HEART

RACHEL V. WEINER

LANDSCAPES
OF THE HEART

LATITUDES PRESS

Some of these poems have appeared in *Caperock*, *Descant*, and *Sou'wester*, and are reprinted here with permission.

LATITUDES PRESS • SINCE 1966

Elizabeth Griffin-Bonazzi, Publisher
Robert Bonazzi, Editorial Director

This book was produced for Latitudes by
On Main Street. The production crew
included Sharon Schiebel and Kathy Perry.

Latitudes is distributed through its international
network by direct mail and through selected distributors in
the United States, Canada, Europe and Latin America.

Write for Catalogs or information to Latitudes Press,
Post Office Box 613, Mansfield, Texas 76063.
Or call (817) 477-1777.

Artwork by Gilda C. Jannuzzi

FOR JOSEPH AND MICHAEL

TABLE OF CONTENTS

III

IV

PYROPHORICS

Lines like these were written
by fire searing the wood
beams sharp as lasers cut
a fire not newburning but prime
raging in its well-borne heat
proud of its sturdy build

and not slow-started but lit
of old ash tightly bedded
dry kindling from the apple tree
pruned last year (even the right
section of the *Times*)
and weighted with trunk pine.

If you wonder why I trouble
to make a fire that would start
anyway, would burn right through
wet hissing timber, let me
tell you that to tend
that hearth is a selfish
chore I do justice to
for the nights it carries me.
That's only fair, you know.

I

THE WAY I LIVE

I'd like to show you the way, but I don't know: it's so
strewn with needles and rocks scattered in tedious
places to trip you, some draped in moss to resemble hillsides,
some piled low on the road to camouflage dips and holes.

In the valleys, I couldn't even count, anymore, how many
layers of stone have slid from the mountains — washed,
purple majesty forsaken, into clumps without design or honor.

I would worry about losing you around the corners:
they're sharp, one-sided angles jutting to the left
or right, looking like sudden dead-ends where a few steps
before, the path seemed open to such interesting possibilities.

There's nearly always another route I have forgotten,
though I suppose anyone else would find it the logical way
to go. I really don't mean to be so obscure. God knows

I've led a fairly simple queue of days, although
carving out markers wasn't the thing I always got done.
Years went by, sometimes, with me sitting up in Faith's tree
swinging my legs at the breezes, talking to no one.

Now shadows, cast from the long windows I stare out of,
are the worst traps of all. As the sun sets, they pattern
themselves on the cracks and crevices of boulders, arch out
like the tall, thick willows my father cut down to make

the parking lot of his store. Some are real, likewise the stones
and the road's shoulders. The pines, shedding centuries
of sweet comfort over the ground, I've imagined entirely.

OCTOBER

Where the Colorado bends and narrows into a smooth
svelte runway the mirror blue of this October sky
we take the children along and drag our gear to the dock
                                          to fish.
It is hours before the late sun rises, before the mist
evaporates, a thin cold friend who sends us back
                              for sweaters and jeans.
On the river, though, it's business as usual.
The fish bubble up between ripples of moss,
frogs catch flies, ducks circle each other, ants mound
into nuisances we must stamp and scratch from
                              around our ankles.
Our taut lines, invisible in the gathering sunlight,
ride the tide, hissing slightly, as do dragonflies,
                        leafbristle, crowflap
and the distant scorn of traffic on the overpass
                        headed to noon.

FLIGHT
DENVER TO LARAMIE

For Blanche Johnson

From the air, the dense green pockets between peaks
        become a map
I can read better than the deepening lines
        of your palm and brow.

At home, I watch you settle into yourself
        like the layers of stone that line the passes.
The day steps gingerly around you
        your eyes, fading, shift from bloom to bloom
                counting the violets on the shade
                        pleated against the afternoon.
Then you leave us for other views.

You try to sew, to read the news, to bring back
        some fervor to the table
        where we wait for you, as we did when we
                were children
        in early from the street for supper
        eyeing the soup still at a simmer.

Or is it you who wait for us to catch up with your
        far-traveling thoughts?
How impatiently you glance back at us
        on the road again, caught in
                a muddle of destinations!

Over the treeless plains, the plain glides
        into an updraft, then plummets.
A current from the west catches us, tossing us
        back and forth until we are rocketing
        through an invisible canyon of wind.

I brace one hand against the window frame
        and with the other clutch
                at my flying baggage.
Even if I dare to look down, I will miss
                (forsake, really)
the windows where you wait to wave us on.

MIGRATING NORTH ON THE AUSTIN HIGHWAY

The fog at dawn draws us close, curving
left and right in slow moves, pulling
the road from under our wheels.
When it lifts, a quick teasing gesture
we see the land, all of a sudden
sharp and clear, glisten like pearls
on white forbidden shoulders. In light
the wildflowers bloom, peerless mantillas
full of grace and the love of spring.

We sleep. Beside us, other men's cloudy
landscapes fade: grazing Braham ghosts
negligible fences, windtowers grey
with the spurious feats of winter.

In the red arms of the sun
the mist rises, for good this time.
I see that we are lost.
The damp road splits open into madly
draped horizons; signs point
everywhere we have yet to go.
For us the days' work yawns toward
ignorant fields: breaking out clods,
turning up pests and pretty weeds
backs already bent toward the fall.

DESTINATIONS

My father is in China now. Across
the shadowed seas he frowns while near him
smiling men converse in thousand-year-old
tongues. Like graves, they spell his name
in musty corners of the room. He nods,
dreaming.

Worry, rage, the ancient scribbling
of the sage attend him here.
But he will spend himself at the bazaar:
gold, dazzling white stars, the jade heart
of Marco Polo preserved until this hour.

He reads his fortune in those incensed
wars, not sure whose voice cries foul
and whose obsequious murmurs send him home.

HOME AMONG THE BEARS

There is a letter behind this tree
folded in neat fours, creases shiny
it has been there so long
and yellowed in one corner
where two or three pine nuts
                age into
dust I could not tell from mine.

                *   *   *

Under the stiff notched trunks
of the sequoia and the corrigated
pine I am home, collapsed
weightless as loose cones on
the hearth and the spirits beneath.

                *   *   *

We waiting for the sun's first flicker
                spring after spring
sleep in their quickening breath
                blue with sprung light.

II

EXPECTING MARCH

As I work an old line, I see from the east window a windstorm
    come up, just in time to clear the air of ambiguous
        warmth, shake from cautious oaks last leaves
            before spring.

This rain whipping in sheets across the trees will, soon enough,
    chill the most interior soul, cringing from vengeance
        letting go hopes we cannot honestly hold in
            dire weather.

Women caught in the streets, surprised at the sudden disturbance,
    turn in collars and chins and pivot home, slipping on
        moistened stones, holding each other, laughing
            between groans.

At the shore, the fishermen grab tackle and run, all smiles,
    to sit under streaming awnings til the setting sun
        glows again on the rarely too bountiful ocean.
            And I,

home already, missing the wet slap of the storm, miles
    from the promising tides, fix a mark of the new
        season on the page, and know it is time
            my child is born.

TORNADO

When it comes, it will rise up
out of the far cornfield
a brazen knot in the sky yellow
as stalks felled after a hasty harvest.

You and I know it's due, know
the wind shifts and atmospheric pulse
that signals things alive: Look up!
Tie down! Take cover! Do what you can do.

The first time, though, we didn't
understand, having just moved from the city.
Pregnant, I took the bus, as usual,
and went shopping in the PX for baby things.

It hit hard, and fast.
The tiles on the ceiling flew up
in a straight path over our heads.
We watched the general's jeep salute
the bowing bank roof and hardly thought
a thing of it, except again
we were lucky.

Now we know. The animals shiver
in the barn. The geese fly low into the reeds
at the end of the smallest pond.
The crows, too nervous to hear inevitability call,
flit about the wide open road, crazy.

I hold you close in my lap
and rock slowly in the still cool air.
Your eyes wander from beams to screen to door
then slide into sleep. Wide awake,
I sing you an old song.

NIGHT WATCH

What must have been an ordinary star
tonight trembles through a green-black haze.
We peer through the lens by turns, my son and I,
puzzling over this fever in the northern sky.
At first we guess it must be Jupiter
promised by the charts to rise soon,
but at its center is a white well, shooting
sporadic rays into the shadows behind the corona.
Over the surface, blue spots nibble fire,
some round as tiny moons, some sinuous
as fat worms exploring spring ground.
"They must be dust clouds, Mom," Joseph says.
"Look how they reflect the fire's light!"

Is this a young nova, a wandering nebula?
Or a fluke in the atmosphere, cluttering
the comforting blackness with delusions?

For a while longer, we relish our find.
The air is cool and dry; the planets hang above
serene and understanding. What we can see
and what is lost by time and heaven's temper
is a dream, beyond imagining, of what we are.

A PICK AND AN AXE

For Joseph

I am down near the low rim with you
where the fir trees are still dark
and full. We are climbing up
out of a deep dream, mother and boy,
but you are at one end of the rope
and I am at the other.
We have brought lots of rope along.

I dig my pick into the side of the rock
where there is no smooth ledge
to pull you to. You are heavy
and you carry your own stuff: an axe,
it looks like, and a shovel.

Where the trees thin, we struggle
along lateral steppes and cracks,
wondering what will hold.

"Hold on!" I yell to you.
We are almost to the mid-plateau
where we can rest and look around.

Already I see the stars you love
shining in a night of glorious tales:
Orion and Jupiter, the Bear, and Cassi
dreaming of tempestuous flight.
Their flames spark the lights in your
eyes, and I name them for what I find:
tears or solitude, or the dimpled smile
from one of those little jokes
you save to tell me at bedtime.

What can you see, from down there?
The night sky edging around the mountain?
The sun chasing it to the other side?
Did you laugh at the frantic eaglet
flapping wildly toward her mother's wing
trying to make it over the horizon?

16

LOOSE

Just when I think I have the morning roads
to myself, one by one boys shuffle out
lean and puffy from unlocked side doors.

They never watch the roads, cross
other people's yards,
then quick and snide merge into traffic
curb to curb.

This time it's spring and the new buds shed
pollen over everything,
light green, like cheap magic powder
smearing drizzle and dust on my windshield.

Before I can shift my gaze
one of them slides into view
hard fist buried in pocket, chin
notched into bony leather blades.

He pulls his sleeve across his face, my path,
                too early to spit
at strangers on the road, or back kitchen
mothers about to serve up steaming breakfast.

LETTER TO J

Here it's rained so hard the roads are waterfalls
embanked by lush green lawns too sensual for me.
Driving through on short errands
I wince at the iridescence of the grass
the houses brassed and vulnerable, and home
the white swing on the patio
just painted, wet and inaccessible.

The yard has overgrown, my neighbors complain.
Mosquitoes and God-knows-what will breed in the beds
and hanging pots. The ivy vines are out of bounds.
Without the dogs to loose, squirrels pelt the roof
and keep the world awake with play.
I lost my job the other day   though
kindly put it comes on me like this rain
and that comma fault in the official letter.

The children are fine. They grow into brown limbs
whipped with fire. They burn their days
trample on wrath, study hatching eggs at school.
Any minute now they will return, one
beating the other home, one flinging the solar system in
(red eye of Jupiter to the fore) on a coat hanger.
We'll find the pond at the park tomorrow overrun with swans
solemn and deliberate, and picnic there.

DIAMONDS AND PEARLS

Last June, my husband gave me this ring
but did not say, "With it I thee wed."
Instead he told me how long and longingly
he searched out a stone of this quality;
still, he wasn't sure he bought the right thing.

The brilliant castle of light is small,
he pointed out, but clear and nearly pure--
only he (and I) and the cutter know about
the crack in one facet, cleverly hid
by a prong in the gold setting I chose.

For a long while, I could not put it on
except for evenings among strangers in town.
It seems a travesty on short, rough, cumbersome
hands like mine who wash and cook and dig
and weather whatever comes, without ceremony.

I wear it now as a signal to the guards
who lock me into day: "Watch out!"
it beams like the ripe pregnant moon
easing over the fitful surface of the waves.
When your backs are turned, I might slip away
into another life, a dreamless, cold sanctuary
in which this ring becomes me, in which
I wear it well, and with pleasure.

THE WIND CHILL FACTOR

For Mike

Half-past suppertime, up you come from the bayou
too clearly stamped with your origins, like a Byronic
couplet we forgot to check for irony.
Hair blowsy, shirt askew, you smile out of the left
corner of your mouth at something in the air
beyond me. You've left your sweater *some*where,
you sigh, flopping down on the sofa and hugging
your legs to your chest. I touch you—you are
pink and hot, skin dry as a far-away desert.

If you were older, you might have come home parched
by love, I think, watching the years escape between us.
Hand in hand down the creek path you two would go
to dream under the willows. Now only a tiny
lady bug caught in your tangles whispers vainly
"Home! Home!" and holds on for dear life as you nod
your head into my worried lap. This time the blush
in your cheeks is a viral revenge. I put you to bed
with remedies as innocent of passion as your sleepy kiss.

WHAT I MISS ABOUT LIFE HERE

There is a dinosaur in my glass
it struts to and fro
shaking its head at the stars
        it glimpses
far beyond the rim of milk.

Each afternoon, the glass tips
        and the brontosaurus leaps out
heading for freedom in the grass.

Here's where you and I come in
        leaping out of our glassy
                winter lives
into rows of fresh-watered cabbages
        carrot ferns, marigolds
feeling our feet again
        as the mud squishes up
                between our toes
and the rocks press their scalloped
        fossils into our heels.

We bend down
        among the elephant ears
to drink from the streams
        the hose-water makes as
wider and wider their rivulets break
        into sturdy tributaries
                bed to bed.

There! a fish darts by, silver
        sliver of sun in the atmosphere.

If this were a clear day
        a long time ago
in our own wide-armed garden

perhaps it would be true
perhaps we would be dancing now
the moonlight full of leaping fishes.

COMMUTING TO THE CONFERENCE
ON URBAN LITERATURE

The door on this on this bus closes all right
but it won't open. Unless the driver
impatient with the suburban stops
gets out of his seat to kick it ajar
the would-be riders like a joke
too early in the morning can't get on.
Though they are saved from the bumpy journey
the repetitious lines and denials
they don't seem grateful. They curse
and rant, gestures almost angry.

By then, though, the bus has reached
the highway and shifts gears. Everyone
seems pleased. In Newark, they search out stops
some slick and glassy, some bombed through.
At a building signed OFFICE FURNITURE
the driver jerks to the curb. *Hey, you!*
he barks at me, *That's yrs.*

IRONING ON SHABBAT

I stop for a moment, brought out
    of my task
by the silence of the house
   emptied of Temple-goers
   emptied of children's banter
     and the noise of machines
that drive the world wild with Saturday
    chores.
Even the grass is still,
rinsing wordlessly into the air
   its dew of dreams.

A prayer flutters before me
     on the board
starched, stiff, a clear form
framing the vision of silence
    like a snowflake
      or a light-limbed speck
of dust. To this, I acquiese.

I draw the hot heavy iron
over the fabric of our lives,
   shaping, smoothing, making them
        well with peace
    this gift of self
on which my soul breathes and rests
  afloat on the smooth board of time.

MOTHER

Coming out of the light
a dark figure framed by the arching
doorway, she opens the night
to wonder, if not peace.
We can hear now
the sound of our breath, rising and falling
thoughts, the fluttery moths
that catch at hope
and die in the flame.

Behind her the air
filters thin and wiry through the screen
the dust settles
the desert hides
   under thick shadows.

In this crater become cradle
she sits among us
  but farther down
on the rickety edge of darkness.

What she dreams
what we might think to say
 into the dark, softly,
evaporates with the heat.
At least we have this, we think between
   sips of freedom,
before even the kitchen window
  goes out.

THANKSGIVING

                                        This time
I would like to be grateful for my hands, seen
in a dash of light through the winter trees
lightly rolling rounds of pastry for the feast
sturdy, plain, coarse and leathery, thick-
veined hands, the sun playing on knuckle-folds,
the wind teasing shadows into a winter dance.

Through the warm quick afternoon after neighbors
have come for breakfast and tea, I turn again
to my cutting and sifting and mixing with extraordinary
humor, so that it shows in the puffy golden looks
I give my children out in the yard, falling

over themselves in the leaves, climbing into
squirrels' territory, heedless of the miracle
of this day: that old and forlorn and badly
chafed, I want suddenly to claim grace
for these unpolished fingers, kneading away at
hope, inventing new shapes for a cranky life

fingers and spirit worn white by this pleasure
heart stilled while hands defy impending hunger

III

METAPHORS

In the first chamber of the heart, there is a cold peace
     of stones waking into the desert morning.
The mountains lift the sun slowly behind them,
     thin rays of light slip through the passes
       like windows on forgotten dreams.
From under a thick alpaca blanket, a smoothwashed sheet,
I lift myself from the pillow of sleep.
On the wide-planked floor, my feet fall silent and sound
       toward morning.

In the second chamber of the heart, there is a garden
        thick with things to pick—
eggplants, beans, tomatoes, squash, basil and sage.
There the earth is warm and dry; it crumbles
     like fussy dough under my fingers.
I make bread, a pie, and heat some soup for lunch on the patio.

In the third chamber of the heart, there is a fire,
an easy chair among shelves dusty with books, a radio
and outside the sea, beating against the shirring sand.
It is winter, white, though not with snow.
Into the mist, cold and wet against my back, I go for wood,
stack the chopped kindling under the eaves, and
think of spring, when we can take our rods down
       to the surf to fish.

In the fourth chamber of the heart, there are stars.
They count the places I have yet to go.
In the blackness, they burn in my soul, flickering
       toward the road,
toward lights from the hotel, toward candles on cafe tables.
In the pale dawn, they melt into wishes, then they are gone.

LIGHT BEFORE DAWN

Before it becomes a pale figure in a pale day

the moon is a white parenthesis, anchoring the clear
            blue anger of the night
to the spike-leaved pinon.

                    My feet firm
the mesa rises to meet them the spirits of my mothers
descend slowly into yellow dust,
                            desert sand,
meal for bread
                    my lover's wild hair
wound tight in my fingers
            when he leaves me
pale arms rising against the sun.

HOMECOMING

between dream and waking
there is a sudden quickness
          in the heart
I touch the thin vein on my wrist
and it taps back to me
a steady, insistent rhythm

in this early, unraveling moment
the song of the night
          the song of the day
are one

          as when the swallow stops
her beating wings
                    mid-air
and turns homeward toward
                    imminent treasons

so she spirals above the lean
          forgotten landscape
so she reins in her silence
                    against time
that enemy of night, of flight
          of clear, long visions

31

GEORGIA O'KEEFE
BLUE LINES, 1916

Out of the same puddle of ink

one
flash-point
leaps lightly toward
the top and
skids open

one drawl
so thin it's nearly
not
bends
where it should have
blossomed
down and away
until only
a backward
look at
its origins
turns it up again
half mast
something to live for.

I think of the second line
more than the first;
one takes for granted
a rod
so straight and tall
it might be anyone's
son, doing
as he ought.

The other, daughter
leans away
finding her life as an echo
draining.
In the end she does
what she can do
skillfully, artfully

whether she was wrong
to go off on her own
like that, wrecking
the parallel opportunity
of two sweet, upstanding
lines, whether
she does,
after all, look like
the guilty one
the bent flower
the broken thought
it doesn't matter

appearances are deceiving
and this is art
which builds
strong impression from deviant lines.

TAOS LANDSCAPE

[*Georgia O'Keefe, 1895-1986*]

In the desert, the colors of day are as pure
as the unbrindled light flicking off the hills
into your eyes. As you walk, a petal's bloom
resurrects itself from the dust into angel's breath.
The purple cast drops onto the canvas. There.

Evening comes. A great trunk looks down at you
swinging under the stars from a low branch
happy and seeing what he is.

Down the dry rocks heat rushes in a gulf
as wide as the Rio Grande; you paint it white
and blue, and show us the fever of longing in a man's
eyes when it will not stop where he stands.
Was it he you lived with all those years?

It must be the loneliness you love—one shell
one fractured skull, the thirsty wildflower
shattering the hard brown door in an adobe wall.
In your hand she is a dark mug of coffee thick
                            with sweet cream.

JOURNAL

Of the things that grow in the dark
I like best the words
that seed themselves among thoughts
like red camelias couched in February snow
or the lone cameleon surreptitious
                              on the night vine
blowing up its pale pink gland
to signal—what?

If danger comes
its stealthy feet
track breath to that very leaf
where we wait
holding at bay what lodges
deep in the underbrush of mind
but turns faithful to light, vision-to-be.

There is the cat
creeping beyond the hedge
there is the thin beam
that transfixes what we know
into eerie shapes beyond name
there is the twisted crevice between trees
the carats of pain winters breed
until like loose-fingered twigs
        aloft on a March wind
they rise up to herald spring.

PERSEPHONE, PAUSING

I am thinking of a new lover
but further than this
I cannot go
     being so long a stranger
       in this wide country
      my head full of filial power
      my eyes replete with his body's
lore.

I take a deep, shivery breath
      and have to ask
where I have come, anyway, that
your stately guard breaks before
my dreams. Like a curtsy, I bring
you scents of the new season.

MISSING THE SHOT

Inside the thicket, the hunter's dream
catches shy glimpses of the open field,
knowing smiles in a distant blind, new
moss (daughter of a bright star) tempting.
Silence unsettles the northern way,
to the south the chase again. So
I am yours.

As if by accident, you walk in
where she feeds, stumbling on an old
root you would have known to find
if you had come this way before.
Your innocence is a mirror of wary
light. You know and don't know.
It leads you.

She leaves these tracks for you.
She learns your sound, the hare hiding
nearby, the turns to take. Already
the boy behind leaps in, distracted
by double gain, too eager to please.
You cry out. The way opens.
She is gone.

From the field, I listen for you
struggling with shelter. I imagine
you packing for home, you surprising
no other deer in thickets, you
wanting sizzling breakfast, bed,
sweet consolation.

HEARTS

Defeated by chance
fifteen and fifteen
only   I see

how the pack
is marked against me
a low pair, nothing wild
the deuce palmed under.

I close my eyes
and dream of you
folding
against the players'
gloating

my hand clasped
to my breast
my heart asunder.

Where is the luck
they promised me
the beginner?
The good girl's surprise
the sharp's inevitable
blunder?

AT THE WOMAN'S CENTER

Have you noticed?
There are three new prints
on the wall. I saw them
arriving last week
under the artist's arm
as we left the room.
It was raining then, too,
has rained every day
since we began
this Wednesday tryst
our muses' words
splattering over us
from the tiny window
and we, happy most times
splashing back.

But the pictures
she brought that day—
what can the woman mean
heating and pressing such visions
into unnatural reds and greens
a blue as unlike sky
as tears, or sparring roads
that don't quite intersect,
mad oceans and volcanoes
hanging in the subtle air
above our camaraderie.

We consider the word.
Pilgrim poet of free love and form,
Whitman wrote that, not thinking,
however, of women at work
nor. . .oh! the pale form
of the child in the last print
hidden behind a vase
of black circles. . .I see her now

elbow hooking the table
leg to her cheek
under the company's feet.

Where could she have
come from, this small phantom
backing into our fears?

DETENTE

I see you have forgotten me
the wild search in your eyes
the tentative smile that grows
and recedes into doubt
your hand cool and limp in mine.
"Oh, yes," you say, "how nice,"
and ask in murmurs about me
since. . .?

You I knew almost at once
by the sidewise slide of your eyes
toward anything else in the room
as if our or any conversation
could imprison you, unjustly
in the here and now. Then you are gone

leaving no wake   no awakening,
not you and I young in a meadow
or the vacant lot, tin refuse
for wildflowers   fast pulses for love
only the diminishing click of your heels
the door that closes slowly — much too
irritatingly slowly — on its rusty hinge.

F.U.O.

I don't know my children
I'm so busy with these arts
and crags   dying
sitting up in bed
    for a miracle
slipping words I would have
shattered the night
        shouting

in the heat of the day
I lie
I lie waiting for a star
to burst like temper
    fired
by an old wound

in the earth
springs like clear
visions
    water shapely green
lives
in the sea
the hawks screech wild-winged
            for the bountiful
fish

What I fear
is a pale fragile
    tiger
lines without meaning
bones with no flesh.

FABLE

I knew an old eskimo who, though
he'd learned his deathsong well,
at the end
            turned ornery and wouldn't
sing. He rowed his raft into an ice
cave and killed the bear inside
for food. He lived a long time
on the meat and skins, gnawing
the carcass bare, then found
a fresh one again and again.
After a while, the young tribe
grumbled at his stubborn age,
his storehouse of silence and frozen
hours. Toothless, he signalled them:
Go! Another herd comes from
the distance. Here death
is one of them.

IV

NOVEMBER
COMING UP BEHIND EAGLE MOUNTAIN
NEW HAMPSHIRE

Wandering wooly across the stones
sunk into the woodside slopes
here comes the lost flock
rambling, rambling.
The winter has them forlorn.
though from the road
we're riding, wanderers too,
they seem to fit the mountain scape
like white stars secure in a troubled plane.

Will the wood take them home again
or do the absent shepherds wait in vain
for sign of their charge?

The heart is needles of pain, bearded cheeks
tear and glisten, iced beyond voice
shamed by the black shadows that crawl
into the afternoon.

BURYING HERBIE IN NOVEMBER

For B.A. and J.S.

Today I sprinkle earth
on this small boy I hardly know
for his mother's sake—his grave
and all his life four measures deep.

That many years ago, we lay
(hearts and wombs in bloom for men
we hardly knew) in beds as white
and cold as this ground's breath
steaming gentle welcome.

With awkward, rusty spade, we dun
the frozen grass which will not die
despite the snow. Still it makes
a point of love for mothers and our
sometime sons.

GHOSTS

Crows flap to the ground
  from bare, burnt ash branches: oh!
wing brushes my arm!

WALKING THE SHORE

These days, they float away from me
sons, pebbles I could have taken home
ships I could have sailed to far ports

light and full, they shine like marble gods
steering sightless toward the heavens

here and there, heavy clumps of mussels
wound in kelp bring my gaze down where
the sand, shifting, draws my shadows

on the surf, strange configurations   men
make of me, not my own rough-hewn soul

not me, flat-bellied Danae
looking out after my fleeing destiny
flashing too late on the pearl horizon.

AFTER A HYSTERECTOMY

I find I do best with ordinary things:
grape leaves stiff and thin on the trellis;
sweet, late-summer winds rustling.
Cordial, the sea-passing of time
and me, my hair in its first grey
the black jetties sunk complacent
in the disinterested waves.
When I can, I walk the boards damp with winter
spray, or watch through a mind-glass
a thousand miles away and see
the same shore, sand packed with old prints
kelp strung among the foam, green sea, white
hopes, tea and biscuits in a box on the nook shelf.

DISCONCERTED

listen: this is where
the music slows to whispers
Time arriving and descent
the scores hung like peeled
ceilings, the turmoil on the floor

windows leap from disconnected lines
that traced them in the dark
where once it was forbidden
symmetry, a room grows corners
and a wall and stings your eyes

ask Homer if there is
a rhyme for moments just before
the dancers leave and the lights
go on: for how the colors make
that dreadful sound.

DREAMS THAT STILL MIGHT COME TRUE

At night I lie in a meadow among the tall bull rushes,
meditating on what I am and where I am going, and find
that I am lying in a meadow among the bull rushes, meditatin
No one can see me, and no one can hear me; it's so dark.